DARE TO BE BAD

A pocket book for all types of artists who want to feel free,
be creative & find the magic within themselves.

MICHAEL LEONI

Published by: An 11:11 Experience Publishing

ISBN: 978-0-692-81927-2

An 11:11 Experience Publishing
Los Angeles, CA
An1111Experience.com

Printed in the United States

Graphic Design and Illustrations by Gracie Wilson.

This book is dedicated …

…to my mentor, Peter Flint who always taught me to "Dare to be Bad". This was his phrase and this book is to honor our work together.

…also to Marsie Standish for teaching me to find my "true self" and my own voice.

…and to ALL ARTISTS who want to be FREE and FIND their "OWN VOICE".

I wish to thank Peter Flint, Marsie Standish,
Michelle Kaufer, Erica Katzin, Ryan Camana,
Alcid Gosselin, Dr. Sarah Larsen, Sharon Gardner,
Jon Pavlovsky, Schoen Smith, Christine Dickson,
Stacia Fiore, Paul Pancoe, Tanje Zammiello,
my parents, my family, my grandfather, Louise Hay,
Eckhart Tolle, Don Miguel Ruiz and all the
artists I've worked with along the way.

THE WORLD IS WAITING FOR YOUR ART!

I

SO WHAT'S HOLDING YOU BACK?
WHAT'S KEEPING YOU FROM
GETTING TO THE NEXT LEVEL?

Being an artist is about
EXPRESSING YOUR TRUTH
— letting the words, the brush strokes, the notes, the dance, the sculpture, come through you from the most honest and vulnerable of places. Many artists have described it as if they're not even in control — they just let go and the 'work' flows through them.

That's the freedom all artists strive for.
So... how do you get there?

3

All of your answers are within **YOU**, but first you need to release the false beliefs and the negative story running through your head that's been holding you back.

THE WORK

Once we understand that our deep-rooted beliefs are the foundation for everything we do and everything we accomplish (or don't) we can start to understand our art (or lack of it) with more clarity. Then, and really only then, can we begin to get out of our own way...

TO ALLOW THE FLOW OF CREATIVITY TO COME THROUGH US.

DARE TO BE BAD!

You cannot find the magic within yourself
or as an artist unless you DARE TO BE BAD!
You must take the risk of being vulnerable to

LET YOUR INSTINCTS SURFACE.

HOW TO USE THIS BOOK

Keep this book in your pocket, in your bag or by your side whenever you're working on your craft or need inspiration. Whether you're in your dressing room before a performance, on set, or an audition, on a photo shoot, in art class, designing a graphic, getting ready to write an essay, a screenplay, a song, a poem, or before a meeting, or a speech...whenever you're being an ARTIST, bring this book so you can be FREE, CONNECT to your HEART and find the MAGIC within YOURSELF.

The first thing you need to do, is take the next two pages and write down all of the things you've heard, or thought about YOURSELF, that have lead you to doubt your SELF as an artist.

GO!

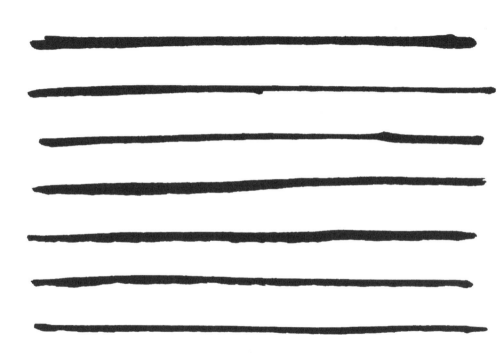

9

10

II

12

Now **TEAR** those pages out and **BURN** them!
RIP them up; throw them in the garbage and
LET THEM GO!
Don't look back. When you throw out your trash you don't
go back and look through it to see what you're
throwing away, you just THROW it out.
All of those comments and criticisms are what CREATED that
negative VOICE inside your head. It's not even YOUR VOICE.
It's a mix-tape of everyone else's trash. None of it is true.
Whatever anyone says about you, or to you, is about them.
IT HAS NOTHING TO DO WITH YOU.

NOW LIST ALL THE REASONS
WHY YOU ARE AN ARTIST.

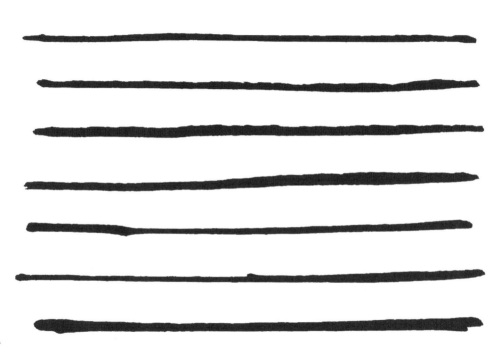

15

16

17

1. RIGHT NOW STOP WHERE YOU ARE. TAKE A DEEP BREATH. TAKE ANOTHER ONE. TELL THAT VOICE IN YOUR HEAD TO SHUT UP! TAKE ANOTHER BREATH AND SAY I AM GOOD ENOUGH.

NOTE: All the conditioning, all of those negative thoughts, are not yours. They're from all the people you've encountered in this life. When you go into your OWN silence, only then will you HEAR your OWN voice. So, say good-bye to all the little friends in your head.

"THERE'S NO GREATER GIFT YOU CAN GIVE OR RECEIVE THAN TO HONOR YOUR CALLING. IT'S WHY YOU WERE BORN, AND HOW YOU BECOME MOST TRULY ALIVE."

– OPRAH WINFREY –

ACTRESS, PRODUCER, MOGUL

2. I AM ALWAYS CONNECTED TO THE CREATIVE FORCE THAT IS WITHIN ME. I CAN ACCESS IT WHENEVER I WANT BY GOING INTO MY SILENCE AND BREATHING.

NOTE: The ANSWERS are within YOU. They are in your silence. They're not on your phone, your laptop or your social media. You can't google it. They're within you. Just you. So, turn your damn phone off!

"I DON'T DREAM AT NIGHT. I DREAM ALL DAY. I DREAM FOR A LIVING."
– STEVEN SPIELBERG –

DIRECTOR

3. MY ART IS A GIFT THAT I'VE BEEN GIVEN.
PLACE YOUR HAND ON YOUR HEART
AND SAY, I AM GRATEFUL FOR MY GIFT,
IT COMES FROM MY HEART,
I ALWAYS CONNECT BACK TO MY HEART.
(Go back & check your list of why you're an artist)

NOTE: All art comes from the HEART.
The HEAD brings the thoughts, the doubts.
The heart connects you to the CREATIVE FORCE.

"NOTHING IS IMPOSSIBLE.
THE WORD ITSELF SAYS, 'I'M POSSIBLE'."
– AUDREY HEPBURN –
ACTRESS

4. I CREATE WITH MY HEART, NOT MY HEAD.

NOTE: our HEART is the connection to the human race. Everyone, whether they want to admit it or not, wants to connect to the HEART. Connection can only happen through TRUE feelings. You cannot think your way to it.

"I AM SEEKING. I AM STRIVING. I AM IN IT WITH ALL MY HEART."
— VINCENT VAN GOGH —
PAINTER

PAST → P<u>RESENT</u>

5. I AM PRESENT...IN THE MOMENT...
RIGHT NOW!

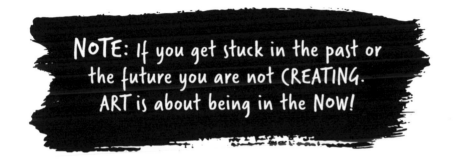

NOTE: If you get stuck in the past or the future you are not CREATING. ART is about being in the NOW!

"DREAM AS IF YOU'LL LIVE FOREVER, LIVE AS IF YOU'LL DIE TODAY."
— JAMES DEAN —
ACTOR

6. STAY IN THE **SILENCE** AND REPEAT TO YOURSELF: I MUST HAVE THE COURAGE TO STAY SILENT AND LET THE IDEAS FLOW THROUGH ME. ALL OF MY ANSWERS WILL COME IN MY SILENCE.

NOTE: It takes COURAGE to get out of our own way. Be brave. Your silence is the path to your TRUE self. (If, by now you've turned your phone back on...
TURN IT OFF!)

"THE POWER IS IN YOU. THE ANSWER IS IN YOU. AND YOU ARE THE ANSWER TO ALL YOUR SEARCHES. YOU ARE THE GOAL. YOU ARE THE ANSWER. IT'S NEVER OUTSIDE."

— ECKHART TOLLE —

AUTHOR, SPEAKER

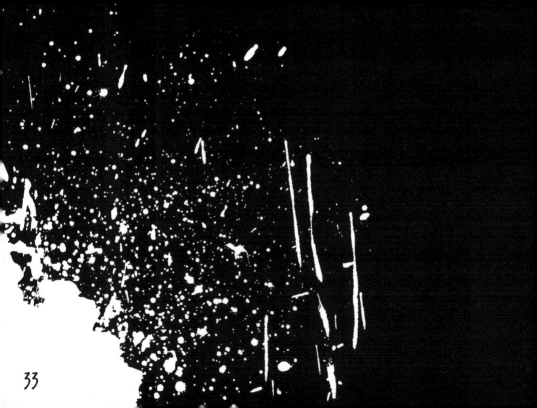

33

34

7. MY PAST IS OVER.
I START WHERE I AM.

RIGHT NOW.

NOTE: All thoughts of yesterday have no POWER now. You cannot be in your authentic POWER if you are stuck in the past. When you step into your artistic space it needs to be a clean slate — the compliments and the criticisms should be left at the door. Trying to live up to past successes, or overcome past failures, will always get in the way of your creative flow.

"THE ONLY LIMITS YOU HAVE ARE THE LIMITS YOU BELIEVE."
- WAYNE DYER -
PHILOSOPHER, AUTHOR, MOTIVATIONAL SPEAKER

8. I WILL STOP CRITICIZING MYSELF.

NOTE: Every time that voice in your head starts to criticize you, REMEMBER — that's not YOU, it's just a compilation of everything you've heard and felt from other people throughout your life...but SURPRISE...everything they've said is what they've heard from other people throughout their life and so on...and so on... Do you see the pattern here? (So tell that voice to SHUT UP!)

"BE WHO YOU ARE AND SAY WHAT YOU FEEL BECAUSE THOSE WHO MIND DON'T MATTER AND THOSE WHO MATTER DON'T MIND."
— DR. SEUSS (THEODOR SEUSS GEISEL) —
AUTHOR

9. I AM WHAT I THINK ABOUT.
I CHANGE MY THOUGHTS,
I CHANGE WHO I AM.

NOTE: Your thoughts have power. Replace the negative with the positive. Listen to what you're thinking, what you're saying. Does it match the artist you want to be?

"EVERY THOUGHT WE THINK IS CREATING OUR FUTURE."

— LOUISE HAY —

AUTHOR

10. I AM UNIQUE, DIFFERENT, AND SPECIAL. I AM ME AND THAT IS ENOUGH.

NOTE: Once you accept yourself it doesn't matter what others think about you. It's their problem not yours. You were brought here for your own purpose. It's your life. Live it fully. If you accept yourself you will not need others to ACCEPT you.

"PUT BLINDERS ON TO THOSE THINGS THAT CONSPIRE TO HOLD YOU BACK, ESPECIALLY THE ONES IN YOUR OWN HEAD."
— MERYL STREEP —
ACTRESS

11. I MUST HAVE THE COURAGE TO
TRUST MY INSTINCTS
AND NOT SECOND-GUESS MYSELF.

NOTE: Don't think, just LET GO! You can never be wrong if you follow your instincts. Instincts are your TRUTH; anything else puts you back in your head. (And that's where those little friends live, and you're not talking to them anymore, remember?)

"HAVE THE COURAGE TO FOLLOW YOUR HEART AND INTUITION. THEY SOMEHOW KNOW WHAT YOU TRULY WANT TO BECOME."
— STEVE JOBS —
INVENTOR

44

12. WHEN I'M IN FEAR I MUST
ATTACK IT. FULL FORCE. NO EXCEPTIONS.

45

NOTE: When you feel the fear, you must face it head on, move through it and conquer it. Once you face your fear, the energy has nowhere to go. It disappears. The only way to grow and expand as an artist is to move through your fear. (So be the Lion, find your courage, and be the king of the forest!)

"EVERYTHING NEGATIVE, PRESSURES, CHALLENGES,
ARE ALL AN OPPORTUNITY FOR ME TO RISE."
– KOBE BRYANT –
NBA BASKETBALL PLAYER

13. I REJECT INTELLECTUAL CHOICES, THEY COME FROM MY HEAD AND NOT MY HEART. I HAVE THE COURAGE TO TRUST MY INSTINCTS AND CREATE FROM MY HEART.

NOTE: Instincts are your truth and your truth comes from your heart. You cannot think your way to CREATIVITY, you have to feel it.

"AUTHENTIC POWER IS BUILDING SOMETHING INSIDE OF YOU, WHICH YOU CANNOT LOSE AND THAT NO ONE CAN TAKE FROM YOU."
– GARY ZUKAV –
AUTHOR

14. I AM AN ARTIST. I DO THE WORK FOR CONNECTION, TO MAKE PEOPLE FEEL SOMETHING.

NOTE: Awards don't matter. The recognitions, the reviews, the little gold man... it's all bullshit. Sure, it may feel great in the moment and give you some validation that you will keep searching for again, and again, and again, but the only thing people really remember is how they FELT when they experienced the art - a painting, a movie, a play, a dance, a song. FOCUS ON THE FEELING.

"I'D RATHER BE HATED FOR WHO I AM THAN LOVED FOR WHO I'M NOT."
— KURT COBAIN —
MUSICIAN

15. I MUST ALLOW FOR 50% OF
PEOPLE TO HATE MY WORK.

NOTE: Once you accept that half the people who see your work will hate it, it frees you. No matter how many awards you get, how many people praise you, you will never please everyone, so just STOP now!

"MY PHILOSOPHY IS... IT'S NONE OF MY BUSINESS WHAT PEOPLE SAY OF ME AND THINK OF ME. I AM WHAT I AM AND I DO WHAT I DO. I EXPECT NOTHING. AND ACCEPT EVERYTHING. AND IT MAKES LIFE SO MUCH EASIER."

— ANTHONY HOPKINS —

ACTOR

16. I MUST BE IN CHARGE OF MY OWN ENERGY. THAT IS THE ONLY THING I CAN CONTROL.

NOTE: The only energy you can control is your own. Let everyone else do what they do. Other people's energy cannot control you if you don't let it. If someone is negative toward you don't return it with negativity; return it with LOVE. The negative energy will dissipate. It has nowhere to go.

"CREATIVITY IS CONTAGIOUS; PASS IT ON."
— ALBERT EINSTEIN —
INVENTOR

THE WORK

17. PLAY! FEEL FREE. BE CREATIVE!

NOTE: We forget to PLAY.
That's what being an ARTIST is all about.
Think about when you were a child, you were PLAYING. You weren't thinking about what your parents or other kids thought.
You were free to just PLAY. (So grab all your toys and jump in the sandbox.)

"EVERY CHILD IS AN ARTIST. THE PROBLEM IS HOW
TO REMAIN AN ARTIST ONCE WE GROW UP."
– PABLO PICASSO –
PAINTER

18. I MUST WORK EVERY DAY ON MY CRAFT.
I MUST BE OBSESSED WITH IT.

59

NOTE: If you want to be an ARTIST you need to be doing it every day, and you should WANT to. If you're not doing the work, it's because you feel you're unworthy of it. Procrastination = unworthiness. ART is your DRUG. USE it!!!

"IF YOU CARE ABOUT WHAT YOU DO AND WORK HARD AT IT.
THERE ISN'T ANYTHING YOU CAN'T DO, IF YOU WANT TO."
— JIM HENSON —
PUPPETEER

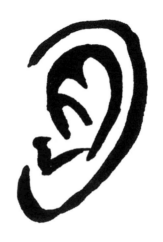

19. I MUST LISTEN. I MUST OBSERVE.
IT IS CRUCIAL.

NOTE: You never know what will INSPIRE you. There are signs and inspiration everywhere. Get out of your HEAD. LOOK, LISTEN, it's all right in front of you.

SIDENOTE: Surround yourself with people that are doing what you want to be doing. (You are who you hang with.)

"THE GREATEST EDUCATION IN THE WORLD IS WATCHING THE MASTERS AT WORK."
— MICHAEL JACKSON —
PERFORMER

20. EXPLORE.
EXPERIENCE ANYTHING AND EVERYTHING.

NOTE: All art comes from experience. What you've seen, what you've learned, the people you've met. It all makes you more free as an artist. Don't say no to anything. (I mean have your boundaries, but, you get what I mean.)

"YOU GAIN STRENGTH, COURAGE AND CONFIDENCE BY EVERY EXPERIENCE IN WHICH YOU REALLY STOP TO LOOK FEAR IN THE FACE."
– ELEANOR ROOSEVELT –
AMERICAN POLITICIAN, ACTIVIST

21. EVERY WEEK DO 3 THINGS THAT SCARE YOU.

① _____

② _____

③ _____

NOTE: The more you do things that scare you, the more the fear energy dissipates; fear will no longer control your life. On the other side of the fear is your authentic power waiting for you to connect to it.
(You had the power the whole time, Dorothy.)

"EXPOSE YOURSELF TO YOUR DEEPEST FEAR. AFTER THAT, FEAR HAS NO POWER AND THE FEAR OF FREEDOM SHRINKS AND VANISHES. YOU ARE FREE."
— JIM MORRISON —
MUSICIAN

22. GET EXPOSED.

NOTE: In order for your ART to be honest, it has to be vulnerable. Do not protect yourself by playing it safe. Everyone wants connection and in order to achieve true connection you must be vulnerable. Only a few have the COURAGE to do it. Be the one that does.

"VULNERABILITY SOUNDS LIKE TRUTH AND FEELS LIKE COURAGE. TRUTH AND COURAGE AREN'T ALWAYS COMFORTABLE, BUT THEY'RE NEVER WEAKNESS."
– BRENE BROWN –
PHD, AUTHOR

23. I AM WILLING TO MAKE AN ABSOLUTE FOOL OUT OF MYSELF.

NOTE: Take the risk. Go THERE! Have the courage not to care what anyone else thinks. (Most people are just thinking about themselves anyway.)

"IT'S WEIRD NOT TO BE WEIRD."
— JOHN LENNON —
SINGER, MUSICIAN

24. I MUST TAKE RISKS.

NOTE: Hiding and looking for protection is the opposite of being an artist. Every great artist and athlete must push themselves. (Muhammad Ali says it all...)

"HE WHO IS NOT COURAGEOUS ENOUGH TO TAKE RISKS WILL ACCOMPLISH NOTHING IN LIFE."

— MUHAMMAD ALI —

PROFESSIONAL BOXER

THE
COURAGE

74

25. I ACCEPT UNCERTAINTY, I ACCEPT THE UNKNOWN; IT IS THE WALK TO FREEDOM.

NOTE: You cannot control EVERYTHING.
So just let go. Be free! Play the game!
It's fun and EXCITING.
When you surrender, miracles happen.

"WHEN YOU BECOME COMFORTABLE WITH UNCERTAINTY,
INFINITE POSSIBILITIES OPEN UP IN YOUR LIFE."
— ECKHART TOLLE —
AUTHOR, SPEAKER

26. I MUST HAVE THE COURAGE
TO STAY IN THE MOMENT.
I WILL NOT LET DOUBT WIN

NOTE: It takes a lot of courage to stay in the moment. The more you do, the more you are in your authentic power. What does this mean? Get out of your fucking head and stay out dammit!

"DEFEAT IS A STATE OF MIND. NO ONE IS EVER DEFEATED UNTIL DEFEAT HAS BEEN ACCEPTED AS A REALITY."

— BRUCE LEE —

ACTOR, MARTIAL ARTIST

27. I'M WORTHY. I'M PROTECTED.
I'M SAFE TO CREATE.

NOTE: You have already burned all those negative thoughts about yourself earlier in this book. Don't go back through the trash. If you've picked up this book, there must be a part of you that knows you're worthy. Stay in that vibration. YOU ARE WORTHY! NOW believe it!

"SELF-WORTH COMES FROM ONE THING, THINKING THAT YOU'RE WORTHY."
– DR. WAYNE DYER –
PHILOSOPHER, AUTHOR, MOTIVATIONAL SPEAKER

28. FEAR IS A LACK OF TRUST IN MYSELF.

NOTE: There is FEAR and there is LOVE.
Which one are you operating in?

"GET THE INSIDE RIGHT. THE OUTSIDE WILL FALL INTO PLACE."
— ECKHART TOLLE —
AUTHOR, SPEAKER

29. I TAKE WHAT I'VE LEARNED,
I SHOW UP PREPARED AND THEN
I BREAK ALL THE RULES.

NOTE: Take all that you've learned, trust that it's already in your body, now **LET GO** and let the instincts surface.

"THE ONLY SAFE THING IS TO TAKE A CHANCE."
— MIKE NICHOLS —
FILM AND THEATRE DIRECTOR

30. FUCK IT!

NOTE: Before an audition, a job interview, a performance, a speech, an important meeting, or just getting ready to CREATE, just by saying those two words, and diving in, you'll be free to be the artist you want to be.

"LIVE LIKE YOU'LL DIE TOMORROW, WORK LIKE YOU DON'T NEED THE MONEY, AND DANCE LIKE NOBODY'S WATCHING."
– BOB FOSSE –
DIRECTOR, DANCER, AND CHOREOGRAPHER

31. FIRST TIME, EVERY TIME.

NOTE: Never try to recreate a moment in a scene you just acted in, or the way you sang a song or danced a dance, or painted a picture, or how you moved an audience in a MOMENT. LIVE IT NOW. BE In the moment like you've never done it before.

"IT'S BEST TO FAIL IN ORIGINALITY
THAN TO SUCCEED IN IMITATION."
— HERMAN MELVILLE —
AUTHOR, POET

32. I AM AN ARTIST... THAT I AM.
I DESERVE TO HAVE A
SUCCESSFUL CAREER.

NOTE: YES YOU ARE!!!!
YES YOU DO!!!
Now all you have to do now is
BELIEVE it!

"SUCCESS IS LIKING YOURSELF, LIKING WHAT YOU DO,
AND LIKING HOW YOU DO IT."
— MAYA ANGELOU —
AUTHOR, POET, ACTIVIST

33. I MUST DARE TO BE BAD.

NOTE: You cannot find the magic within yourself or as an artist unless you DARE TO BE BAD! You must take the risk of being vulnerable to let your instincts surface, and connect back to your HEART.

"ONLY THOSE WHO DARE TO FAIL GREATLY
CAN EVER ACHIEVE GREATLY."
– ROBERT F. KENNEDY –
AMERICAN POLITICIAN

But...

one last thing

PUT YOUR HAND ON YOUR
HEART AND ASK YOURSELF

"WHY AM I SO AMAZING?"

Use the next few pages to write down your answers. Take as much time and space as you need to answer this question. Make it a continuing practice.

97

98

99

100

THE WORLD IS
WAITING FOR YOUR
ART, FOR YOU TO
DARE TO BE BAD.

NOW GET OUT
THERE AND DO IT!